CONTE

INTRODUCTION...................................... er

SIMPLE BEGINNINGS......................... ..3

MOTORISING AN EFE LEEDS HORSFIELD 7

AN EASY WORKS CAR 13

WHITE METAL MODELS AND PLASTIC KIT CONVERSIONS 21

TRAMWAY DIORAMAS..33

STARTING A LAYOUT. 37

SOURCES OF INFORMATION AND SUPPLIERS 45

For the best in tramway modelling join the Tramway and Light Railway Society. It is the only national society for tramway modellers. For details send an SAE to the Membership Secretary, 6, The Woodlands, Brightlingsea, Essex, CO7 0RY.

Front cover:- Model of Liverpool Tramcar number 762, one of a dozen Preistly bogie cars built with English Electric mono-motor bogies. The original tram is undergoing restoration at the Birkenhead Tramways depot. The model is a Tramalan conversion kit using the Tower unvestibuled E/1 plastic kit. Model built by Alan Williams and seen on his layout.

Rear cover:- London MET 'D' Type, one of the last open top tramcars to run into central London. It is shown on the small diagram built using the Airfix 'Monty's Caravan' kit.

© David Voice 1997

ISBN 0 9529937 0 8

Published by:
David Voice Associates, 9, Redwing Court, Kidderminster, Worcs., DY10 4TR.

Typeset and printed by:
Forsyth and Steele, 161, Blackpool Old Road, Poulton-le-Fylde, Lancashire, FY6 7RS.

The complete motorised Birmingham Radial tramcar from the Alphagraphix card kit. The wheelbase of the power unit is about right. Luckily the overlarge wheels are mostly hidden by the sideframes.

The power unit straight from the 'HO' diesel locomotive. The three axles, sideframes and couplings need to be attended to.

CHAPTER 1

SIMPLE BEGINNINGS

An aspect of tramway modelling that can seem daunting is painting a complex livery. Well this has been solved in a range of card tram kits produced in 'OO' gauge by Alphagraphix. All these kits are printed in full colour and can be bought at pocket money prices. They make a good way to start off in tramway modelling.

There are over 20 different 'OO' gauge tram card kits in the Alphagraphix British range. They cover many different cities and towns. The first task is to choose the tramcar you want to build. My choice was kit TC10, the Birmingham 'Radial' 4-wheel balcony tramcar. A four wheel car is easier for the beginner than a bogie tram and as I live near Birmingham there is a local connection for me. In addition this tram has quite a long wheel base, which gives more flexibility when motorising it.

The next task is to find suitable power unit. Now the whole idea of this project is to keep the cost to a minimum, so I selected the power unit more on cost than on accuracy. If you do not intend to cut out the windows of the card kit you can use the whole of the inside of the tram for the power unit. While it is nice to get a unit that is close to the wheelbase of the tram, it is not essential as most of it will be hidden. This also applies to the diameter of the wheels.

This means that bogies from 'OO' or 'HO' diesel locomotives can be used. I have included 'HO' because often second hand model locomotives based on European prototypes can be found cheaper than British models. If you are not sure about small electric motors, either get a friend who does know to help you buy one, or go to a model railway shop who will ensure that the locomotive does work. Model railway exhibitions are useful places to find inexpensive diesel or electric locomotives and they can be tested on a nearby layout! Do not forget that the worse condition the body is in, the cheaper it will be and that is the bit you will be throwing away. If you are used to small electric motors then any source can be used. I purchased my locomotive from a car boot sale. Since it was not possible to check it, the price I paid was on the assumption that it was a non runner (I actually bought it for the pantographs and only paid £1.50). When I got it home I found that the motor was a good runner, which tempted me into this project.

I made up the card kit following the instructions, except that I left the interior empty. I do recommend that you take the little extra time to colour the edges of the card during assembly using felt tip pens. This makes an enormous difference to the look of the final model. As this was intended to be a quick model and I was using a massive power unit, I did not cut out the windows. If you are willing to spend more time in order to create a detailed model then the windows can be carefully cut out and glazing added using clear acetate sheet (used by lecturers for Overhead Projection presentations), or clear plastic card, glued inside the body. If you do cut out the windows then you should complete the job by adding interior detail, particularly the seating in the upper saloon and some representational seating in the lower saloon to hide the traction unit. If this is your plan then the traction unit will have to be much smaller than the one I used from my second-hand diesel. See Chapter Two for suitable small traction units.

Having finished the body shell I looked again at the locomotive traction unit. I removed it from the locomotive body (disconnecting the wire from the trailing bogie). I had decided I would make this model for two rail supply. There were three jobs that had to be done before the bogie could be used. First there were three axles (six wheels) so the central wheelset needed to go; second I had to sort out the pick-ups in order to get the electrical supply to the motor; and finally I had to have some way of attaching the unit to the tram body.

The removal of the central wheel assembly was simple. Under the unit there was a plastic keeper plate which I unclipped. The axles were plain to see and it was just a matter of taking out the central one. As only the outer axles were driven by the motor this worked out very well. The keeper plate had the bogie sideframes moulded onto it. So I cut these off with a sharp knife and clipped the keeper plate back in place.

The electrical supply was a little more complex. The power bogie picked up power from one rail, the other side was completely insulated. In order to get the power from the second rail the locomotive's trailing bogie was used. As this was not going to be part of my tram I had to think of another way. If I had been making the model live overhead I would have just connected the wire from the trolley pole to the second brush on the motor. However, I wanted two rail, so I needed to get a pickup from the insulated wheels to the motor. I glued a piece of copper clad paxolin (actually a cut down length of 'OO' gauge copper clad sleeper) onto the keeper plate. Then I soldered a length of nickel silver wire (the same as I use for the overhead) so that it touched the metal back of both insulated wheels. Finally a short length of wire was soldered to the copper clad and connected to the second brush of the motor. It was given a quick test run to check that all was well.

The top of the motor was a strange shape that bore no relationship to the interior of the tram body. So to provide a method of fixing I glued some card strip the same width as the motor to the sloping sides to form two triangles, with a straight top that was just the height of the interior of the tram body. As a bonus I found that the tumble home of the lower saloon was just right to squeeze the power unit in place and the tram could be picked up without it dropping out (though it was loose). So I have been able to put the traction unit in place without gluing it, and I am able to remove it easily at any time should the need arise.

As I was making this as simply as possible I followed the instructions for the trolley pole, so it is non working. When I finished making the card kit and fitted the power unit the model was ready to operate on any model railway type track. For a more realistic operation it would be practical to make street tramway track and overhead. A working trolley pole could be fitted to the roof of the tramcar. As the trolley pole can set up severe strain on the roof, some stiffening, like 40 thou plastic card, would need to be glued under the centre of the roof.

The finished model gives a very good representation of a Birmingham tramcar and the whole thing cost me less than £3. Now I cannot guarantee that you can be as lucky as myself over the power unit, but I am sure that you could make a fine working model tramcar for around a fiver.

ting pick-up wires to the wheels. A short piece of copper clad paxolin is glued to the base and a gap cut in the copper. The wires are thin nickel
ver and the pick-up from the insulted wheels has a wire a wire leading to the motor. The current from the other wheels is collected from one
le, hence the need for the pick-up wire to connect the wheels.

e complete card kit and the power unit. This shows just how big the unit is. The top of the unit has the card strip glued on the allow the unit to
st in the correct place inside the body of the tram.

Also from Alphagraphix is this kit for 'Bluebell' the experimental bogie built for the Metropolitan Electric Tramways in London.

Alphagraphix have this Glasgow 'Coronation' class tramcar in the range of 23 different 'OO' gauge card tram kits.

CHAPTER 2

MOTORISING AN EFE LEEDS HORSFIELD

The Exclusive First Editions (EFE) diecast model of the Leeds Horsfield was the first ready built model of a British tramcar in 4mm scale and for many years was the only one. available. At the time of sending this book to the printers I have just heard that Corgi have announced that in the Summer of 1997 they are introducing a die cast 4mm scale tramcar in their Original Omnibus range. It is of the Blackpool bogie streamline Balloon. I look forward to exploring how to motorise it when it is available.

Here I must just say a word about diecast tramcar models. There are two other manufacturers who have made diecast tramcars. Matchbox was the first and they made a typical open balcony 'Preston' type four wheel car. However, the scale they chose was 'HO', 3.5mm to the foot or 1:87 (4mm scale or 'OO' gauge is 1:76). When placed against a 4mm scale model of the same design of tramcar the Matchbox model is noticeably smaller. This is unfortunate because the model is very nice. I have seen a British 'HO' layout that uses repainted and motorised Matchbox tramcars which are very realistic. The advantage in the 'HO' Gauge is that there are many correct scale scenic kits available from the continental market. However, the disadvantage is that it is not possible to use any of the many British 'OO' gauge tramcar kits on the layout, because of the difference in scale.

The other manufacturer is Corgi, who make four types of the basic 'Preston' design. They are the totally enclosed body, the enclosed top with no vestibules (windscreens), the open top car and a single deck tram. These all use the same range of parts and so have a very common look about them. I must put in a word of warning. Corgi have put out in their publicity material that the trams are 'OO' gauge. This is correct in that the models are sold with a track gauge of 16.5mm. However, they do state on the boxes that the model is 1:72 scale. My own measurements put the scale at 1:64, which in model railways terms is 'S' gauge. At this scale, the 16.5mm track gauge is exactly right for 3'-6" gauge tramcars. Again I have seen motorised versions of these models and it is practical to built a layout. However, there are few, if any, scenic models in 'S' gauge and again British 'OO' gauge tramcar kits would look very out of size against the Corgi trams. If you are proposing to motorise a Corgi tramcar then remember that Model Tramcar System (see information at back of book) can supply a ready made trolley pole to the correct scale for the roofed tramcars.

Since my book is firmly in the 'OO' gauge camp I will confine the rest of the chapter to the EFE tramcar. This is a superb, exact scale replica of the Leeds Horsfield tramcar. At the time of writing models seem not to be available in most shops . The latest model, in a khaki livery with mesh windows, sold very well. Earlier versions of the model have been made in red, light blue and dark blue liveries. Thankfully these can still be found, particularly at swap meet sales and at the National Tramway Museum, Crich.

When motorised and fitted with a working bow or trolley pole the finished model is superb and there is the added benefit of not having to paint the model! So starting with the traction unit the first job is to select which unit you will use. There is a choice of four, two ready to run and two in kit form. The tram has an 8'-6" wheelbase, which scales to 34mm. Looking at these in the order of price, most expensive first. The first option is a slight

The EFE Leeds Horsfield in wartime khaki livery straight out of the box.

Under the tramcar, showing the plastic bushes that hold everything together. The left hand bush has been drilled for removal, while the right hand bush has been taken out showing the end of the steel rod.

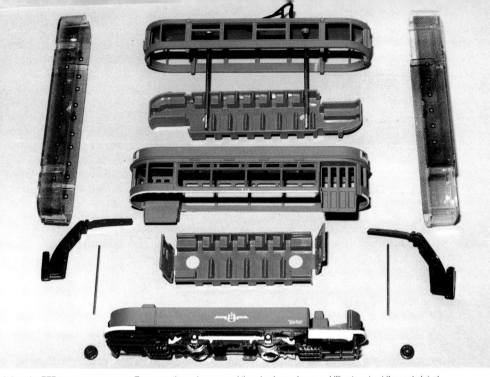

This is how the EFE tramcar comes apart. To remove the under gear and the wheels needs some drilling to cut out the central rivet.

The floor has been prepared by cutting a rectangle first in the plastic chassis and then the diecast floor.

compromise as it uses the 31mm wheelbase Tenshodo. Sold as a motor bogie for model railways, it actually is just right for many four wheel trams. The Tenshodo comes in several wheelbase lengths, the 31mm being the longest. The next ready to run chassis is the Bec traction unit. Bec offer many sizes of traction unit from 24mm to 36mm in 2mm steps. The 34mm is right for the Horsfield. If you want to construct your own chassis from a kit (very useful for learning about traction units) there are two on offer. Both require some soldering, so if you have not tried soldering before this is a good time to learn. It is not hard and once you have the technique you will also be able to erect overhead. The first kit is made by ABS and uses a white metal chassis. ABS do various size four wheel traction unit kits and one especially for motorising the EFE. The final kit is an etched brass traction unit from David Voice (ex-PC), with a compensated axle which can be made in any wheelbase from 30mm to 36mm.

The next job is to get into the model in order to make the necessary modifications. Looking inside the tramcar you will see two bright metal rods running from the roof to the floor. Turning the car upside down you will see the ends of these rods in the keeper plate. In fact each is kept in place by a plastic bush, which is a force fit onto the rod. These have to be removed. In the early days of EFE models I used to hack them away leaving a pile of small bits where the bush used to be. Now I am more advanced and remove the bushes whole as they come in useful later to hold every back in place. So I drill four small holes (about 1mm diameter) into the bush, just touching the rod. These relieve the pressure and the bush can be prised off the rod in one piece, ready to be used to hold it all in place. Put them into a safe place, with the handrails. I Sellotape mine to the inside of the top deck roof. When the bushes are removed the model falls apart, though the plastic keeper plate is still in place. This is removed by drilling out the rivet in the centre of the underfloor. When the splayed top is drilled off, the keeper plate can be removed and the wheels fall out.

One of my tricks is to place all the bits into an old ice cream tub. This keeps them safe. I only take out the bit I am working on. Then if any of the smaller items (like the stairs) should fall off, I do not lose them. Take the bottom of the tram and cut the plastic underneath with a sharp craft knife along the back of the trucksides, from one of the rectangular holes to the other. Then cut from the rectangular holes across the tram to the circular hole. A rectangle of plastic should drop out. Now the same size piece of die cast floor has to be removed. I drill a hole about 1/8" diameter in one of the small recesses in the floor. Then either open the hole out with a file or drill a couple more in a straight line, so that I can fit a junior hacksaw blade into the hole. Take care during this operation not to scratch any paintwork. I use a piece of cloth to hold the body and kept removing all swarf every few seconds, as it can be very abrasive.

I cut the hole to size using the junior hacksaw blade. I was going to put the body (well wrapped in cloth) into the vice. When went into the garage I found that it would have take longer to clear a path to the vice than to do it entirely by hand, which is what I ended up doing! So if you have very little equipment you can still do this conversion. I held the body in my left hand and sawed with just the blade (no hacksaw frame). This allowed me to be careful about the paintwork. It only took a few minutes to make the necessary four saw cuts. Inevitably they erred on the cautious side, so the final job was to file the hole to the correct size. I did this the same way, by holding the body in my hand. I soon had a good rectangular hole in the floor.

The choice of power unit is up to you. On the left is the Bec ready to run traction unit; next is the plastic bodied ready to run Tenshodo power unit; then the ABS traction Unit kit; and finally on the right the ex-PC etched brass traction unit kit.

The ex-PC Bow kit made up and mounted on the roof of the EFE Leeds Horsfield tramcar.

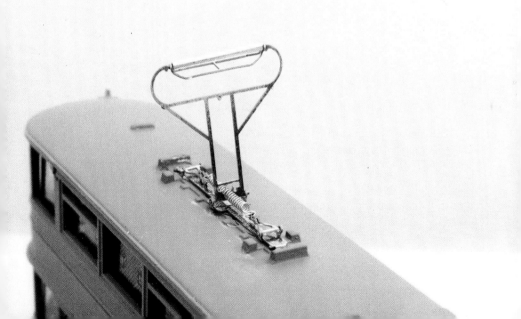

I next made the traction unit kit. I used my own, ex-PC kit, which I made to 34mm wheelbase, following the instructions. I had to cut the main plate of the chassis to fit in the hole in the tram body. I used a slitting disc in a hobby drill, but a razor saw could also be used. If you are not going to re-use the plastic bushes to hold the body back together, then you can cut a larger hole in the lower saloon floor. Though it will then be necessary to glue the parts of the tram together.

Comparing the chassis to the tram body it was evident that some more room was needed in the lower saloon. So I took the plastic seating moulding and cut about 4mm off the tops of the bulkheads. When I tried it back in the tram body I found it did not move upwards as much as I thought it should. On looking closer I found this was due to the window moulding holding down the sides of the seating. Using a junior hacksaw I cut down either side of the seating backs about 3mm. The seating moulding slotted in nicely and when I put the chassis in it was the right height. I glued a small piece of balsa wood under the seating at each end to lift the seating moulding to the right height.

The chassis was kept in place in the most simple way. I stuck a piece of double sided sticky tape on the chassis and this holds it in place under the seating moulding.

Next I looked at the roof. The plastic bow was removed by cutting off the plastic rivets from the inside of the roof. The bow lifted off the roof. I made up a David Voice scale bow collector kit, using the Leeds type of skid plate counter balance and long base. At the ends of the base there are two fixing tabs. I drilled holes in the roof for these to fit into. One tip here is to stick a piece of masking tape over the roof before drilling. This stops the drill from wandering and if there is a slight slip there is less chance of getting a scratch. I fitted the finished bow in position with a dab of super glue. If you want to make your model live overhead then solder a thin wire to the longer tab. You may also need to drill clearance holes in the top of the upper deck window moulding. I painted the base of the bow collector grey and the rest of the bow (except the spring and skid plate) black.

Reverting now to the underside of the tram, I cut the lifeguards from the base plate moulding. These were cut so as to allow them to fit over the holes for the bushes. The final job was to assemble all the parts. Make sure that you get the seats the same way round, you do not want the top deck to be going the opposite way to the lower deck! I used the bushes to hold it all in place. If there is any movement a dab of super glue on the steel pins before sliding on the bushes will hold them securely.

Your model is now ready to run on the layout.

CHAPTER 3

AN EASY WORKS TRAMCAR

Some of my most enjoyable times in tramway modelling have come from taking an unlikely model or kit and making a reasonably representative tram from it. One such project was described in my first book, "How to Go Tram and Tramway Modelling" and was a works car made from an Airfix meat wagon kit. In "Tramway Modelling in 'OO' Gauge" I included a photo of a small works crane trailer made from a coal staithes kit.

In this chapter I will be describing how I made a works car from a cheap Ertl toy. It all started when I was in the Forge Shop at The National Tramway Museum, Crich with a German friend of mine. He was looking at the Thomas the Tank Engine models stand and suggested that the well wagon with the Traction Engine could make a tram works trailer, as there had been some similar trailers in Germany. I was not so keen as I could not recall anything like that in Britain, though the railways used well wagons to move tram bodies from factory to customer.

Near to the well wagon was a pair of oil trucks in bright yellow with "Sodor Fuel" on the side. Now many British tramways had water tank wagons that were used to spray water over the track. This was for three reasons, the water would damp down dust in dry weather; it acted as a lubricant between the metal wheels of the trams and the rail, which was particularly useful on tight curves; and the water helped with the electrical continuity between trams and the rails. At their simplest the water wagons consisted of a water tank on a chassis with an open driving platform at each end. Some systems put a simple roof over the tank whilst others enclosed the tank making the tramcar look like a stores van.

In making my model I chose to make a water wagon that was unmistakable, so there was to be no van body. I also decided against the roof and I went for the plain tank on a chassis. The final decision was that it had to be motorised, as all British water cars were self propelled.

After purchasing the Oil Wagons (they come as a pair for about £3.99) I took one out. I was pleased to find that the mouldings were held together by two screws, rather than the usual rivets. After unscrewing them I found that the model came apart into five pieces. The tank, with the end beams glued on; the upper chassis; the lower chassis; and two wheel sets. Your first decision is whether to make your model motorised or as a static model for a display in a depot. For a static models carry out the actions described below but instead of modifying the chassis to take the motor, you will be able to use the existing parts.

Put all the parts in a small box for safety, an ice cream tub is ideal. Take out the upper chassis and cut away the lugs carrying the axles. The plastic is quite soft and the main part can be cut with wire cutters. I made the bottom of the moulding smooth by using a very sharp wood chisel to scrape away the excess plastic. I cut away the buffers and then took off the projecting base of the buffer beam, using the chisel again. The solebars of the chassis contain detail that is more appropriate to railways and tramways. So I sanded the side smooth, starting with a medium/fine grade paper and finishing with a very fine paper to give a smooth surface for the paint. The upper chassis is now ready for the driving platforms

13

The Tramalan LCC wheel carrier works car stands next to the unmodified Thomas the Tank engine Sodor tanker wagon.

Having taken the tanker wagon apart, the floor is cut and the tramcar platforms and dashes added. The floor straight from the wagon is the top one and the converted one if shown below.

to be fitted. Cut two pieces of 40 thou plastic card 19mm long and 22mm wide (adjusted to just fit between the side beams). These are glued using a liquid polystyrene glue, with 5mm under the chassis. There must be a clear 54mm between the plastic card rectangles to allow the motorised chassis (the David Voice, ex-PC kit) to fit.

The dash plates are simple rectangles with rounded upper corners and made from 9mm by 22mm, 40 thou plastic card glued on the ends of the platforms. To strengthen the platform and the dashes glue another rectangle of 40 thou plastic card 11mm by 22mm on the top of the platform. A strip of 10 thou plastic card about 2.5mm wide is glued along the bottom of the dash to represent the fender.

The headlight is a circle of 30 amp fuse wire 4mm inside diameter super-glued to the dash. I wrapped some fuse wire round a paint brush the right diameter. Then I cut the wire to size with a sharp knife and used pliers to make the wire into a perfect circle The next parts have to be purchased. These are a pair of white metal trucksides. For the small cost they save hours of detailed modelling and are well worth it. The wheelbase is up to you. I used an 8'-6" wheelbase with roller bearings representing a fairly modern truck (on the basis that the tramcar would have been retrucked at some stage in its life). For a motorised version I would recommend using between 7'-6" (the minimum wheelbase of the chassis kit) and 8'-6" wheelbases. See Information Section at the end of the book for suppliers.

I used Bec trucksides and found that they fitted behind the side beams giving just the right height for the chassis. I did need to file a small nick at the ends of the upper extension pieces to clear the plastic card platform. I super-glued the truckside in place. I now found a small gap between the main part of the trucksides and the soleplate of the plastic chassis. From my workbox I took a suitable size strip of plastic (many years ago I bought a packet of mixed sizes plastic strip which is still going strong and proving invaluable) and glued it in place. It then looked like a piece of channel girder that had been placed to raise the tram body slightly.

I next turned my attention to the tank. Luckily not much work was necessary. I filed the top of the central filler cap flat and drilled a 1/8" diameter hole in it for the brass socket of the working trolley pole. I used the David Voice (ex-PC) trolley pole kit, made up following the instructions. I cut the length of the pole wire to 55mm during assembly. I glued the brass socket into the tank and put the trolley pole assembly in a safe place until the model was finished. To finish modelling the tank I filed and rubbed it down with fine wet and dry paper to take away the worst of the moulding joint mark and the "Sodor Fuel" marking which otherwise would be seen through the paint.

I next made up the traction unit. For those not sure about assembling a traction unit kit, it would be possible to use a Tenshodo ready to run traction unit. A large hole will need to be drilled in the centre of the upper chassis moulding to take the upper boss of the Tenshodo unit. As this will be hidden by the tank there should be no problem. If you use the ex-PC kit then make it to the wheelbase of the trucksides you have chosen. The chassis was built following the instructions, taking care to ensure that there was no binding of the gears. I filed a small notch in the end of the upper plate to take the assembly screws, which will hold it all together. Finally I painted the sides of the motor black (to hide it better behind the trucksides) and put the traction unit safely to one side.

Although there were still many detail parts to go on, I decided it was time to paint the main parts. I painted the tank and the chassis a matt maroon (Humbrol matt 180) all over. I was not sure how well the paint would take to the shiny plastic so before painting. So I brushed the body all over with liquid polystyrene glue. This gives a better surface for the paint to bind on to, but make sure you do not handle the model until the glue is absolutely dry, or nasty finger prints will be left. After the paint had dried I decided to spray the final coat. I use Halfords acrylic car paint sprays. The colour I had handy (left over from another tramcar model) was Ford Lacquer Red (No 453050). I hung the tank by pushing a cocktail stick into the trolley hole and using a wire and crocodile clip to hang it up. The chassis I sprayed on a sheet of newspaper. As it had to be sprayed from above and below it took a little longer.

There was nothing further to do on the tank, so that got put to a safe place. The chassis now needed the all important detail. I find that it is detail that makes a good model. It does take time, but if you are able to compare a highly detailed model with a more plain one the difference is astounding.

So first I painted the platforms grey and the inside of the headlights white. The trucksides were painted matt red oxide (I use Humbrol matt No 70). The fenders were painted gloss black, as were a couple of commercial white metal controllers (which then had a gold painted top). You could make the controllers from a small piece of wood sanded to shape with a plastic card top and a short wire handle. After painting it is very passable. The handbrakes are simply brass wire bent to shape and glued behind the dash, on the driver's right. Under his left hand I glued the controller in place. The driver, from Bec, was painted matt black with flesh coloured hands and face and glued on the platform with his hands on the controller and handbrake.

Works cars were numbered in many different ways. Sometimes they were included in the normal fleet numbering, sometimes they were numbered in a separate series. London County Council (and the London Transport) gave them a number starting with 0 (hence 01, 02 etc.). In Birmingham they had PW in front of the number to signify "Permanent Way". I decided to follow the London system and numbered mine 01, with the 0 and the 1 either side of the headlight. I used the gold/red shaded numbers from the Blackpool transfer sheet sold by Tower Models (a superb source of numbers, not just for Blackpool). To give the tramcar an extra bit of detail I decided to add 'legal lettering' This is the name of the general manager. Mabex (see information at the end of the book) make a white transfer with legal lettering for buses. To convert these to trams all that is needed is to cut off the unladen weight. The tiny writing shows the wording "General Manager" clearly, then is obscured for the actual name.

Next the drivers steps were added. I made them out of 40 thou brass wire bent to shape. I made both steps each end from one piece of wire which I glued under the platform. Then the lifeguards and life-trays were added. These can be made from plastic card (though in my experience they are very prone to breaking) or soldered from very thin brass strip. To save myself time on this model I used white metal castings from Bec. The lifeguards were epoxy resin glued to the trucksides. Since the platform is rather high I super glued two pieces of brass wire bent to an "L" shape alongside the vertical bars. These were then glued under the platforms, between the wire of the steps. This effectively lowered the lifeguards slightly. I painted all the under gear red oxide.

Underneath the made up ex-PC power unit kit, with the chassis shortened ready to fit the water tramcar.

The chassis of the works tramcar ready for painting and then having the tank fitted.

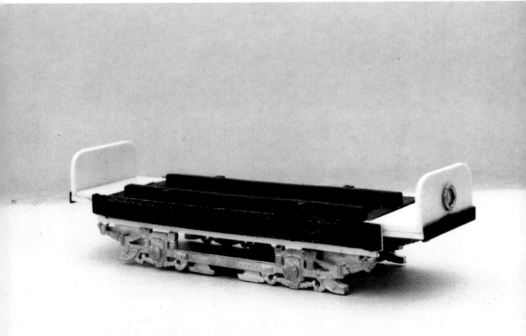

The complete works tramcar on the layout. The livery is relatively simple, so I think it is necessary to put on the detail like the General Manager transfer and the simple steps. The driver helps to add the finishing touch.

I take my ideas from wherever I can get them. Alan Kirkman was the first modeller I know who used the Dreadnought kit to make the Lytham St Anne's single deck trams. This is his model on his Lord Street, Fleetwood layout. I am sure that the Lytham trams never got that far north!

I put the tank on the plastic chassis then placed the motorised traction unit in place. I put a Peco insulated washer (the 'OO' large size) on each screw and put them in place. I found it best not to tighten them up too much as the traction unit tended to distort. So I screwed them up until the traction unit just held in place.

The final job was to paint the trolley pole black and put it into the brass socket in the top of the tank. Then I put the finished model on the track, ran it and stood back in admiration!

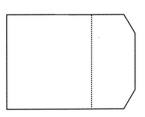

DIAGRAM 1

The platform for the Lytham tramcar shown full size. Cut two from 30 thou plastic card.

DIAGRAM 2

Pattern for soldering the wire to form the lifeguards. After soldering file a flat on the outside surface and then bend the bottom wire and uprights to form the final shape.

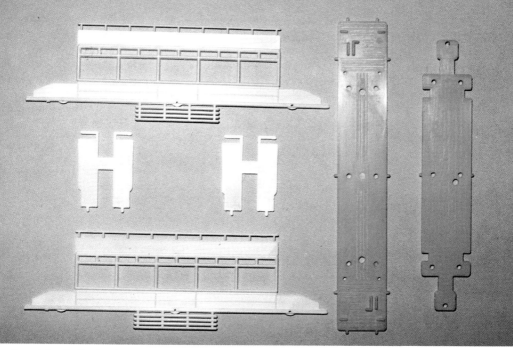

The parts from the Dreadnought kit that are used on the conversion.

Sides ends and the floor with the hole for the traction unit. Note the brass wire used to make the waist rail.

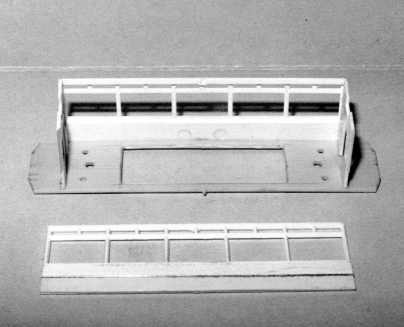

CHAPTER 4

WHITE METAL MODELS AND PLASTIC KIT CONVERSIONS

Soon you will be wanting to make models of your favourite tramcars. Here the very wide range of white metal and plastic tram kits from different manufacturers are invaluable. At the time of writing there are 40 different white metal and 12 different plastic British tramcar kits and a further 25 conversion kits available. The manufacturers and suppliers are listed in the Information Appendix. I will not cover the assembly of these kits as they all have very comprehensive instructions. You should note that the plastic kits are produced as static models and no provision is made for motorising them. My book "Tramway Modelling in 'OO' Gauge" gives full details on getting four wheel and bogie kits running.

Despite the very wide range of kits available, at some stage you will want to make a tramcar but there is no kit. My first suggestion is to look at the existing kits and see if there is one that can be converted. One of the most enjoyable aspects of the hobby for me is working out how to convert a kit from one particular tramcar into some entirely different. Indeed at one time I ran a competition for the best conversion from the very first plastic tramcar kit, the Blackpool Dreadnought. It really was amazing what was done and some wonderfully inventive models were made.

It was this wish for more tram kits that led Tramalan into producing a range of conversion kits. These kits use a variety of the plastic kits and with special white metal parts the plastic kit can be converted into a quite different tramcar. Thus the Blackpool Vambac can be converted into a trailer set, an OMO or even a Boat. The Tower London E/1 can be made into Bolton 66 or the Hill of Howth tram. A Bournemouth bogie car can be made from the Tower SHMD open to car.

I would suggest that for your first conversion you try altering a plastic kit. The reason for this is that you will feel more free to cut and change a £5 kit than one costing around £30. For this chapter I will describe how I changed a bogie open top Blackpool Dreadnought into a single deck four wheel Lytham St Anne's Corporation tramcar which may well have run alongside the original Dreadnought trams in Blackpool. Four of these tramcars were purchased second hand by Lytham from Dearne and District where they were part of the standard tramcar of the fleet. As with all modelling it is essential to have good photographs to work from. The book "The Tramways of Lytham St Anne's" by P.H.Abell, J.A.Garnham & I.McLoughlin, published by The Oakwood Press contains excellent photos of these tramcars.

Apart from the livery the description of the conversion can be used to make the original Dearne and District tramcars. The whole fleet consisted of 30 of these single deck trams. When the Dearne and District system closed in 1933 4 of the trams were sold to Lytham and a further 5 were sold to Falkirk and District Traction Company. The Falkirk cars were altered quite radically. First the gauge was altered to meet the 4'-0" gauge of the Falkirk system. Then it was found that the tight curves in Falkirk necessitated shortening the trams by 3'-3" and the trucks to 7'-4" wheelbase. This is quite possible to make, but the parts will need to be altered to fit the Falkirk requirements. The book "The Tramways of Falkirk" by Alan Brotchie contains photos and details of the modifications made on the actual cars.

The Dreadnought kit has a special place in the hearts of tramway modellers. It is the very first 'OO' gauge plastic kit of a British tramcar. Though of an unusual prototype the kit has proved very versatile and many models of other tramcars have been built using parts from the Dreadnought kit. So the techniques described in this chapter can be used to modify other kits into other types of tramcars.

The items needed for constructing the model are the Dreadnought plastic kit, some plastic card 15 thou, 30 thou and 40 thou thick, plastic strip 0.5mm by 0.75mm and some from a mixed sizes pack. White metal castings of 8'-6" trucksides, destination boxes and headlamps. Brass wire 20 thou and 30 thou diameter. A traction unit kit and a trolley pole kit (for both I used my own ex-PC kits). Optionally you may want to get a driver, conductor and passengers.

Opening the kit I decided that the parts I was going to use were the two sides, the two bulkheads, the lower saloon floor and the upper deck floor. I put the rest of the kit into my bits boxes, or should I say one of my many bits boxes. I never throw anything away, because it is bound to come in useful on a future model. I started the modifications on the sides. Since the Lytham car is a single deck tram I needed to cut off the upperdeck decency panels. The beading above the windows proved handy. I cut the panels off with a craft knife, using the beading as a guide. I find it useful to start with light cuts, making sure that the cut goes exactly where I want it. Having got a groove I then could press harder and with several strokes cut through the plastic. The craft knife was also used to cut away the dog gate under the side. Next I used a junior hacksaw to cut away the extensions flush with the ends of the lower saloon. The next job was to tackle the panel below the windows (known as the rocker panel). The Dreadnought has a flat side with a lot of beading, while the Lytham car has an angled rocker panel with a single beading (the waist rail). So I first cut away all the beading with a craft knife followed by sanding the side smooth. Then I cut a strip of 30 thou plastic card 5mm wide and the length of the side. I sanded a chamfer along one edge and then glued the strip in place immediately under the window with the chamfer on the lowest side. Then I cut a 6mm wide strip of 15 thou plastic card which I glued below the first strip. To form the waist rail I took a length of 20 thou brass wire and glued it along the joint. To glue the wire in place I used Evostik impact adhesive. As with all glue take care not to spread any over the surface of the plastic.

The next job was to modify the bulkheads. I marked out the windows either side of the door. These are 5mm wide and 10mm high, with the lower edge at the same height as the lower edge of the other windows. I drilled out several holes in the window and then made the hole to size using a craft knife and file. Then I filed an archway to the top of the doorway. Finally I cut the top away to the height of the tram sides. Then I turned to the floor. The platforms of the Lytham tram are much shorter than the Dreadnought, so the original floor can be used. I marked where the bulkheads fit and then marked out the position of the hexagonal dash. The drawing shows the size needed. The junior hacksaw was used to form the correct shape. Next I cut a rectangular hole 60mm by 20mm in the centre of the floor to allow the traction unit to be fit. Again I drilled some holes and then used a craft knife and file to form the hole.

Now that the main modifications had been made I assembled the sides, bulkheads and floor to make the main form of the tramcar. I used my normal form of assembly, that is leaving the roof to the very end. This allows me to have full access to the interior of the

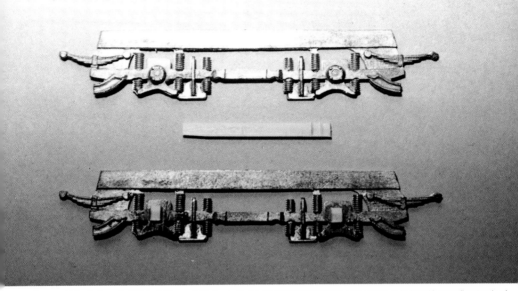

A small but crucial detail. The only 8'-6" trucksides available have roller boxes. By filing the round boxes off and replacing with a small rectangle of plastic card you get a much earlier form of truckside.

The model is really taking shape. The body and most of the parts have been painted. The roof, truckside and fenders are all ready to fit. The unpainted parts below the trucksides are the strengthening pieces to go as ceilings for the platforms, giving extra rigidity to the ends.

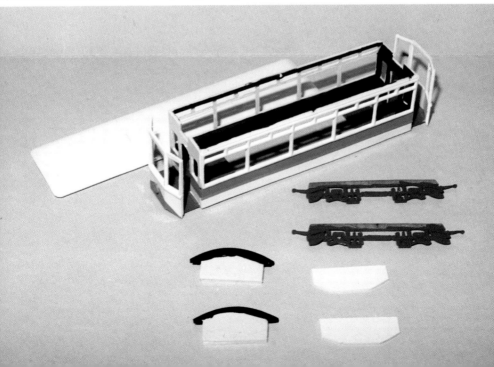

The lifeguards and dog gates soldered in one part from brass wire and bent to shape.

The complete ex-PC trolley pole kit, ready for painting black.

The tramcar in service with a few passengers. This is quite a simple conversion, yet is so different from the plastic kit that provided the parts.

Another conversion, a Great Eastern Grimsby and Immingham tramcar from two Bachmann American Brill trolleycars.

Starting the depot diorama. The engine shed sides and end are in place, the rails glued to the board and card has been fixed in place to form the depot floor.

The engineering part of the depot diorama. The motorised truck is the only 'OO' model of this sort I have come across. The shaft driven lathe and drilling machine come from the Will's Finecast workshop set.

saloon for painting, glazing and fitting the traction unit. After leaving at least 24 hours for the glue to properly harden, I then cut away the strips of floor either side of the hole. This is to allow the cast trucksides to be glued in place later.

The next parts to be make are the ends. Now there are a variety of ways of making this and I certainly would not claim that my design is the best, but it suits me. If your favourite method is different then do use that. The ends are made from plastic card. Now I find that I never make a neat job of cutting windows in thick plastic card. So for this job I used 15 thou plastic card and cut the end with the three windows. Note that the height of each window is different. I scored down the joint of the three panels and bent the end to shape. This I glued to the edge of the platform. Now 15 thou is rather fragile, so to strengthen it I glued panels of 15 thou plastic card inside and outside the dash. Then I used 0.5mm by 0.75mm plastic strip to form the beading around each window both inside and out. A wider strip was glued above the central window. Above the front offside window there is a light. I represented this with a pin head. I drilled a small hole in the panel and cut the head off a pin and glued it in place. The finishing touches are the headlights, where I used Tramalan white metal castings. Alternatively you can use a length of 30 amp fuse wire wound round a 3mm diameter rod and cut to make a complete circle. Then glue it in the centre of the dash.

The vestibule assembly looked a little fragile, so for additional strength I cut two pieces of 40 thou plastic card the same size as the platform to fit immediately under the roof. I did not glue them in place yet, as I wanted the access in order to paint and glaze the inside of the vestibules.

I then started on the roof. I thought that the original Dreadnought upper deck floor would form a good basis for the roof. I cut the extension pieces off and then checked that it fitted inside the saloon. I had to file a little off to get a good fit. The I cut two rectangles of 40 thou plastic card about 0.5mm wider on each side than the tram. Mine were 31.5mm wide and 131mm long. Yours may be slightly different as your assembly might be a little different from mine. Now the ends of the roof are very square with the corners rounded. I curved mine about 4mm radius, I used a small washer to draw around and then filed the curve. Next I glued the first rectangle over the upper deck floor. My first mistake was to keep the floor the correct side up. The moulded wearing strips on the floor prevented a smooth contact. So I gave that up and after letting all the glue dry off I turned the floor up side down and glued the smooth sides together. This worked. I did check very carefully to make sure that the roof sat squarely. Then the second rectangle was glued over the first. The roof is now 2mm thick and the final shape was made by sanding with medium sand paper and a firm block and finishing with medium grade wet and dry paper to the required profile. One word of caution. The plastic dust produced has a high static charge and sticks to anything and seems to get everywhere. I do the sanding over a sheet from an old newspaper which I throw away with the dust on it. To get all the dust from the roof wash it under running water. Actually this is a good tramcar for this technique, as the roof is very flat and not much sanding is needed. When the roof was ready I cut a 30 thou plastic card rectangle 5mm by 50mm to form the trolley plank. I marked lines along the centre lines of the roof and trolley plank. These were used to glue the plank accurately on the centre of the roof. Before painting I drilled a small hole (about 1mm diameter) through the plank and roof in the centre of the plank. This was to locate the trolley position after painting. Again the roof was not glued in place yet as I wanted to keep the access to the inside of the saloon clear for painting and glazing.

I painted the roof with two coats of matt white enamel. Then I finished it with a coat of gloss white. I took the opportunity to start painting the body of the tram at the same time. I painted the whole of the outside, the inside of the dash and vestibules and the outside of the bulkheads with two coats of matt white followed by one of gloss white. Then I masked off for the light blue. I have described this in detail in the companion volume "Tramway Modelling in 'OO' Gauge" so I will not repeat it here. The blue I used was Humbrol matt 89. I also painted the inside of the saloon dark brown and the floors mid grey, while the headlamp was picked out with gloss white.

After a couple of coats of blue and removing the masking I started on the transfers. The coat of arms came from Mabex. I had some old dry-print gold transfers which were small enough for the name on the sides and the number. Mabex also do small water slide transfers which could be used. Building up a long name out of individual letters is never a favourite task of mine. This tends to show in the finished model as the letters wander about with a will of their own. You can probably do a better job than me. When all was in place I gave the outside of the tram a coat of gloss varnish for protection.

Next came some small parts. I started on the trucksides. Now the only 8'-6" truckside commercially available is the ABS/BEC one and it has roller boxes. Now there are four choices. First use the truckside and turn a blind eye to the incorrect roller boxes, second use an 8'-0" truckside and ignore the smaller wheelbase, third take a smaller truckside cut it down the middle and stretch it to 8'-6" by adding new bars and fourth file off the roller boxes and replace with plastic card square boxes. I decided on the last of the options and I filed off the round roller boxes. I cut a short strip of 40 thou plastic card 3mm wide. I filed a 45 degree slope along a long edge, between the top and the edge. I took about 1mm off the top and the side. This formed the sloping part of the axle box that forms the top of the box. I cut four 3mm long pieces off the strip, each piece being square. These I glued over the filed off roller bearings, using Evostik. When painted they make a good representation of a square axle box. When the glue was dry I painted the trucksides red oxide. I also took two controllers and a driver and conductor and painted them matt black. The controllers I finished off in gloss black with a gold top and the staff stayed matt black with flesh colour for the face and hands. The handbrakes are the vertical wheel type. I purchased Bec brake wheels and glued them on to a length of brass wire with a short right angle bend at the top. I painted the brake wheels a brass colour. Then I glued all these parts in place.

The next job is to glaze the windows. I like to use acetate sheet (the sort used for Overhead Projectors). This is very clear and gives a high reflection which enhances the model. For the saloon sides I used the moulded windows as patterns and cut a rectangle of glazing and glued them in place. Use a small amount of glue on the very edges and be careful not to smear the window. If this happens it is easier to scrap the window and make a new one than to try and clean it. The windows in the vestibule were cut individually and glued in place. Then I cut a couple of 5mm wide strips of 15 thou plastic card the length of the saloon. These I painted dark brown and glued them on the floor to represent the longitudinal seats. The floor is raised to the height of the seats. To hide the high floor I painted four people, cut them at waist level and glued them to the seats. This helps make the eye stop at the windows and not look into the tram to see where compromises had to be made.

Being rather cautious I still did not glue the roof in place. I drilled a small hole dead

A simple scene that sets off the Glasgow standard to its best. Made from super quick low relief kits and a short piece of road. This was made by Helmut Gieramm who took the photo.

'HO' not 'OO', but with such character that I could not resist it. This is a freelance depot with Vienna tramcars and made by the late Peter White.

centre in the roof where the trolley pole fits. I decided to use the ex-PC trolley pole kit that I supply. This requires a little soldering. I made it up according to the instructions. Then I opened up the hole in the roof to fit the trolley pivot bush. I glued this in place and the trolley was slipped into position. It is a loose fit and can be removed later for painting black. As my car was to be two rail I did not have to complete the electrical connection to the overhead wire. If your tramcar is to be live overhead, solder a lead to the trolley pivot bush before gluing it in place. Run the lead under the roof to a corner and then fit it down the corner and under the floor. Have some slack before soldering the end to the motor brush in order to be able to remove the mechanism for maintenance. To complete the roof add the destination boxes. Here again commercial items are used. To adapt them I glued small strips of plastic card at each end to form the 'legs'. I painted the assembly two coats of matt dark brown followed by a gloss varnish. The boxes were fixed on the roof with super glue. For the destination blind I prefer to use a printed blind rather than hand paint. Over the years I have accumulated a wide selection. Tramalan and Tower both do Blackpool blinds, but none of the destinations were quite right. Then I found a coach destination sheet with 'Blackpool' on it, which was one of the Lytham destinations. Failing that you could take the 'Gynn' from a Blackpool destination 'Gynn Square'. It is a bit short, but is better than a shaky hand painted blind.

The final parts to complete the tramcar are the steps, lifetrays and other undergear. Now steps can be very fragile. So I decided that I would make them strong rather than exactly to scale. The easiest way was to cut a strip of 40 thou plastic card the width of the steps and glue it under the two layers under the platforms making the fenders. Then a rectangle of 15 thou plastic card was cut as wide as the steps and the length across the tram from the outer edge of on step to the other. This I glued under the three layers with the end sticking out forming the steps each side. This looks good and gives plenty of strength.

The lifetrays are cast commercial items from Bec, painted red oxide and glued to the ends of the trucksides. Again strength is required as they tend to get knocks, so I like to use a good blob of epoxy resin, which is painted red oxide when set. Finally I made the lifeguards and dog gates. These I soldered up from 30 thou brass wire. The drawing and photos show the construction. To hide the fact that wire was used I filed a flat surface on the outside after soldering it all together. The front two uprights fitted into holes drilled under the platform while the side dog gates were supported by bending the uprights under the floor. Everything was fixed using epoxy resin, then painted red oxide. You can now add handrails from brass wire as the final detail.

Now the finished model is ready to take its place in your fleet. Like all new trams it is best to give it a chance to run in, with a little oiling and adjusting if things seem too tight or too loose. I have trams that do regular service on my layouts that I built twenty years ago and they are just as good as the time that I finished them all those years ago. One of the things that I do is to paint the finish date of the model under it. This gives an accurate means of telling the age of the model. Though I must say it also reminds the modeller of the passing years!

The doyen of dioramas is Peter Huxford. This charming scene, full of atmosphere is just a few inches square. The tramcar is made from a Tramalan kit of the single ended Rotherham tramcars, one of the few single ended tramcars ever found in this country.

My 'OO' gauge layout in an A4 box file. Not very realistic, but fun to make and to run. No one can say they have not got room for a layout this small.

A little larger and admittedly 'HO' gauge, is this superb continental layout by Don Sibley. Giving a continuous run and the interest of a depot in 3 ft by 18 inches.

A detail shot of the depot on the same layout. ETM stands for Elektrische Tramweg Maatschappij.

CHAPTER 5

TRAMWAY DIORAMAS

Having completed a model tramcar there are now a few things that can be done. It can be put away in a box, but that seems a pity as neither you nor anyone else can enjoy it. Of course you can display it at home, which is nice, though do take care where it is put. You do not want it to be knocked off a shelf. Ideally it should be in a glass case, which will help keep the dust off it. Model trams are not the easiest things to dust.

Obviously the very best way of seeing your models is to run them on a layout. However, not everyone has either the space (though tramway layouts can be remarkably small) or the inclination to make a layout. So how about a diorama? This not only allows the model to be on show, but it also places it in context, like the layout does. Now dioramas vary greatly in size. So I will describe a few that range from a little larger than the tramcar to almost small layout size.

Now the very smallest display feature is a little bit of track. The Hadfields kits include a small straight length of roadway and tram track. So the tram can be placed on this track when being displayed. While this helps to place the tram in context (the street) it is rather too small to make much impact. The next step is a diorama that is a little larger than the tramcar itself. The simplest I have come across was an idea developed by Peter Huxford. He used some parts from the Airfix kit of Monty's Caravan. The kit contains a small diorama of a road junction with a damaged statue and tram tracks. Now some modification is necessary to enable the tram to look right. However, the finished diorama is just 140mm by 111mm. I actually mounted mine onto a piece of wood 150mm by 125mm. I put a gang of workers clearing the statue, with the obligatory foreman watching. It would be possible to remove the fallen statue completely and perhaps restore it using a model figure. The idea is just to create a small scene, preferably with a piece of action to give added interest. The road should be a dirty brownish-bluish grey with rust coloured 'rails' a black grating and a more bluish curbing stone with stone paving. Although there is no overhead, the scene is still very attractive when the tram of your choice is added.

The next step up is a small scene of your own design. Again Peter Huxford has made quite a few of this type of diorama. A rectangular piece of plywood around 200mm by 175mm will prove to be an excellent base. Now one of the key features, that Peter has used with great effect, is to make sure that the tram track is not parallel to the sides of the base. Peter sets his at a slight angle and uses the board to make a junction of the roads. You will have the opportunity to try out road building techniques (as described in my previous book "Tramway Modelling in 'OO' Gauge"). The pavements need to be modelled and after that you can let your imagination go. One that Peter made had a set of traffic lights at the junction and the rear pavement had a wall with an advertising board, of the right period of the tram of course. There is an enormous amount of street furniture available from many model railway manufacturers. Etched brass gates and railing can also be used to good effect as well.

A slightly larger type of diorama can be used to create more of a scene. Peter Huxford built a most attractive scene of the inside of a tramway depot and I copied the idea, with my own ideas on details. The base can be of anything you have to hand, plywood, plastic, as long as it is stiff and will last. I found an offcut of 9mm thick MDF (Medium Density Fibreboard) and cut that to size. Next I got a Dapol (ex-Airfix) plastic kit of the engine shed. The idea is to use the two sides of the engine shed together to form the back of the diorama. So the board needs to be just long enough to take the two sides and the ends. My board is 284mm long. I made the board wider than the engine shed to give extra floor area in the depot. The width of my board is 108mm wide.

I made up the walls of the depot from the engine shed by gluing the two walls together to make one long wall. I then glued the end with the smaller doors, making sure that the outside of the walls (ie with the brickwork markings) was actually put on the inside of the depot. I cut the front end (with the large doors) vertically up the edge of the doorway, to give a small section. I then painted the whole of the inside with three coats of white paint. The windows and small doors were painted green. While the paint was drying I laid the track. I cut two lengths of rail (I used code 70, but you could use code 100) the length of the board. These I glued to the base so that they ran to the centre of the end wall, with a gauge of 16.5mm (remember gauge is measured between the inside edges of the rails). I built up the floor using thick card. As the rails are straight this is quite an easy job. Once laid I painted the floor medium grey.

I fitted the windows and doors to the walls then glued the walls in place on the board. I decided I wanted to represent the overhead wire, but this gave me a headache. At the back of the depot the end wall formed a good anchor point, but there was nothing at the front. I soon realised that part of the problem could be solved by using Plastruct 'U' channel upside down to represent the wooden boarding used in depots to protect the overhead wire. This meant that I did not have to put any tension on the overhead. Next I found that the kit had a roof truss frame for use when extending the shed. I glued a piece of 'I' girder (more Plastruct) across the roof truss and the end wall. As I had some parts left over from another engine shed kit from a previous project I was able to put a second truss at the centre. I then glued the channel in place. I painted the truss and trunking a dirty brown.

Then I painted the outside of the walls a matt black. I used the lamps in the kit (plus an extra one from the spare kit) by painting them green with white bulbs and glued them in the holes provided (adding an extra hole in the centre of the side wall). I put the notice board in place (painted brown), gluing it in the place left for it on the wall. This completed the basic diorama. The next stage is to me the most interesting and that is adding lots of detail, or in the case of the depot, clutter. As the walls were painted white the depot bay is really the paint shop. As such it would probably be kept clear and clean. The likely detail would be ladders, paint pots, a cupboard for paints, brushes and so on. Peter did this on his diorama, complete with a part painted tramcar. However, I wanted something different, so my bay represents a paint shop that has been changed into an electrical and blind repair area. So at the end I was able to add some machinery from the Workshop Set (SSA M102) offered by Will's Finecast. This is superbly detailed and I found it irresistible. I also added a blind table from thick plasticard mounted on 2mm rectangular section plastic making the eight legs. A notice (a modified railway item) was glued to the notice board.

To give the scene a focus I decided to model something I have never seen in 4mm scale, a complete four wheel truck with motors. I started with cast white metal trucksides from Bec, which I cut and filed until just the truckside was left. I had some of the PC very

Another simple layout consisting of a single oval of track with a length of double track at one end. With automatic operation this is ideal for exhibitions, allowing the operators plenty of time to see the other layouts on show! Made by Alan Kirkman using Alphgraphix card bullding kits it was completed in a minimum of time. For added interest the bus operates on the Faller road system.

The other end of the same layout, showing the reserved single track. The red lorry is operating on the Faller road system.

fine scale tram wheel sets which I adjusted to 16.5mm gauge. I drilled holes for the axle ends and mounted the trucksides onto the wheel sets. To represent the motors I cut two short lengths from a hexagonal section pencil. I cut some card, drilling holes for the axles, which I shaped to fit over the ends of the pencil. One end is larger than the other, to represent the gear cover. I used four lengths of brass wire to make the motor support bars and the 'X' bars in the centre of the truck. The top and bottom bars on each sideframe were added from plastic strip. I cut some plastic card to make the lifetray boards. I painted the motors gloss black and the rest red oxide. I placed the finished truck at the end of the track with a couple of spare wheel sets.

The Wills Workshop Set has three workers, so these were added. Then the rest of the clutter was positioned. This rather depends on what you have in your scrap box. I placed a long destination blind on the table, using double sided Sellotape. As can be seen in the photos I added destination boxes, trolley bases, wheelbarrows and a bicycle.

On an entirely different theme and for the 1995 Festival of Tramways Exhibition Ron Howes and John Prentice were inspired by the theme "Trams at War" to make a diorama of a London tramcar having been damaged by the blast of a bomb. Based on an actual incident in the War the diorama caught the atmosphere of the event very well, with an ambulance in attendance and ARP wardens clearing the scene. This leads me to another thought. I have yet to see a diorama of a tramcar accident. Luckily there were few actual cases, but those that were often had much media attention and often postcards of the accident would be sold.

Moving up a size the next type of diorama is really rather like a piece of layout. I have built a London conduit change pit on a board 600m by 225mm. This has a backscene with shops and houses and could at some future stage be built into a larger layout. I have also incorporated the overhead. So something like this can give you experience of all the techniques needed for a full working layout.

I hope that this has sparked off some ideas for you. Certainly dioramas allow your imagination to explore all kinds of modelling possibilities which are attainable in a realistic time scale. I am sure that there are many more ideas yet to be explored, so why not have a go?

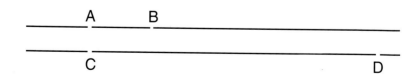

DIAGRAM 3

The cut rail technique for automatic operation. All rails are electrically bonded except for AB and CD which must be completely insulated from all the other rails and each other.

CHAPTER 6

STARTING A LAYOUT

Dioramas are fine for displaying your model tramcars. However having made your models I am sure you will want to see them running. This will mean either making a test track or a layout. Test tracks are useful items to have. I have one that is a yard of flexible track with a couple of tight 'S' bends to give a good check for clearances of a model. Others I have seen have been small ovals. It is best if the test track has an overhead and a continuous oval does give the chance to run the model for a while to ensure the chassis beds down nicely.

In between a test track and a layout is an operating diorama. From the last chapter you will have gathered that I am a great fan of dioramas. Indeed if the diorama is made long enough then it can also act as a test track.

Of course layouts are the ideal answer because they give the proper setting for a number of tramcars to be operated. When thinking of a layout the first thought must be what size to build the layout. There are no rules about this, it all depends on the space you have available and what you want to use the layout for.

First the space. My first tramway layout fitted on top of a chest of drawers in the spare room, though now I store them in the loft. I have also built a layout in the loft, which gives a nice run. I have also seen storage shelves used for an end to end layout and even coffee tables. Indeed tramway layouts can be fitted into incredibly small spaces. I built an 'OO' gauge layout into an A4 box file, while Ralph Price built an 'N' gauge layout on a board 18 inches by 18 inches. End to end layouts can be fitted onto boards just 6 inches wide. On the other hand a wonderful Black Country layout was built by Malcolm Till on two boards 8 ft by 4 ft set at right angles to each other in his spare bedroom.

This takes us to the use of the layout. Now this can cover a large number of things. My original layout was built as a test track and a photographic background for my models. Yet its greatest use was as an exhibition layout and yet it was just luck that it happened to fit into that role as well. So the first question is "to exhibit or not to exhibit?". If you want to exhibit the layout then you must give consideration to two aspects.

1.   It must either be small and light enough to carry and fit into your vehicle, or it must break down into parts that are as convenient. In my experience 4ft x 2ft is the maximum size for easy transporting and if you can make the boards smaller then that is better.
2.   It must provide reliable and continuous movement. The public want to see trams moving. not standing still. So I would suggest either a layout with at least one continuous run or an automatic end to end.

Even if you are not thinking of exhibiting I would still recommend that you design the boards so that they can be separated and are small enough to carry out of the room. After all you may at some time in the future move house!

Lol Reeves has made a small rabbit warren of a layout, with narrow street and corners not curves. Once described by a tramway model manufacturer as impossible, Lol proves otherwise and the many exhibitions where the layout gives reliable service, entertaining the public. The layout also features the names of many well known midland tramway modellers.

Not sure about overhead? Well Lytham St Anne's had gas tramcars in the very early days, as did Neath. This interesting layout was built in New Zealand by Syd Naish. The tramcars are heavily converted plastic kits. Photo by Syd Naish.

The West Midlands Group of the Tramway and Light Railway Society decided to build a small layout to demonstrate modelling techniques and to be able to display an operating tramway on publicity stands at exhibitions. The size of the layout was determined at 3 ft by 1 ft. On the board will be an end to end run and a depot. I think most modellers could fit such a small layout in their house somehow.

On the basic design there are three main categories. There is the end to end, which I have already mentioned and which is how most prototype tramways operated. At its simplest it could be a single track and this could be fitted onto a board just 2 inches wide. Using a commercial backscene like Peco or Townscene even scenery can be added. Of course only one tram at a time could be run. To make it a little more interesting some or all of the track could be doubled and again it is possible to use a narrow board. The absolute minimum is 3 inches, but I would recommend around six inches. Two exhibition layouts based on the end to end are "Lord Street Fleetwood" by Alan Kirkman and my own "London's Tramways". Both layouts are one foot wide and have boards 4ft x 1ft. These are very easy to handle, fit well into cars and give plenty of space for scenery. However, there is one word of caution. If you are modelling a system with trolley poles, then either you will need to hand turn the poles at each end, or you need to build a trolley reverser, which is an impressive, though complicated, piece of overhead. In the case of the layouts I mentioned the London layout represents the conduit and the Fleetwood layout is set in the present day with pantograph equipped trams.

The next type of design is the continuous oval. The minimum board width for a single oval is around 14 inches, while for a double oval I suggest 20 inches. This gives a radius of 7 inches for the inner track and 8.5 inches for the outer track. My first layout "British United Tramways" was just this. By electrically breaking each track into six sections I was able to operate up to ten trams. Now that automatic operation is more favoured for exhibitions Alan Williams has built a similar layout to run six tramcars automatically, three on each track. This gives plenty of continuous movement while allowing the model trams to have short rests to prevent motor burn out when running all day.

The way in which live overhead tramway layouts can use automatic operation is simplicity itself. We can take advantage of the fact that the current supply can come from the live overhead. Using a live overhead and bonded wheels and rails it is possible to use the rails themselves as a switching device. For a tramcar to be at the stop and a following tramcar release it and then itself halt at the stop just requires four cuts in the rails. The diagram shows the method. The rail lengths AB and CD are electrically isolated from the rest of the track. If you make your own track from copper clad sleepering then you will have to cut the copper cladding off the sleepers attached to rail CD. A tram on rail AB will not move as both rails are electrically dead. When another tram approaches and passes point D its bonded wheels allow the current to flow across to rail CD. This becomes live and allows the first tram to power away from the stop. By the time the second tram reaches the stop it is clear and on reaching rail AB the second tram halts. It is as simple as that.

To run three trams on a single oval two such stops are needed, one each side of the oval. The three trams will then run very happily two at the stops and one moving, with the three changing places at the stops. For the casual observer it all looks as if highly complex electronics are being used.

No your eyes are not playing tricks. This layout by Ron Deamer does fold up for transporting. The buildings and backscene have been positioned to allow them to overlap to keep the folded layout to a minimum size. Choosing central London and the conduit again means no overhead. When opened out a model house fits over the hinge to hide it. Photo Ron Deamer.

The Lickeys turning circle on Ralph Price's Birmingham layout. Though it seems some standard gauge cars have managed to pay a visit. A turning circle like this on a large layout provides an excellent place to park plenty of trams.

Don Piggott's Wednesbridge is a layout so full of character it takes ages to fully appreciate all the features in it. Typically Black Country, the buildings provide the ideal backdrop to the tramcars.

Capturing all the atmosphere of the old Black Country is this corner of Malcolm Till's "Tamebridge" layout, modified for exhibition service by Ralph Price, with his Birmingham 365 taking the bend.

There is a third type of layout and that is the out and back. Here there is one terminus and a turning loop. So the tram leaves the terminus journeys around the loop , returning to the terminus again. This type of layout does not readily lend itself to automatic operation and like the end to end would also need hand turning of the trolley poles after each journey (unless the trolley reverser was used).

No matter what type of layout you decide to make there is one important rule. Always put in more track sections than you think you will need. It is easy to cut the rail and solder a wire to it during construction. If you do not want to use the section immediately then just connect the wire to the controller. At some stage in the future you may want to run more trams and that means more sections. It is simple then to disconnect the wire and add a switch. The only other way is to dig up the road surface and add the break later, which is a far from easy task.

Track laying and overhead has been covered in my previous book "Tramway Modelling in 'OO' Gauge". So I will not repeat myself here. However, it is worth remembering that careful design of the layout can   simplify construction and operation. For example I designed my London end to end layout so that four of the five points are sprung, so I only have to operate one point. This will work for many designs. Certainly anywhere that has single track with passing loops can use sprung points. In the case of single track and passing loops, the overhead can also be made more simple by using a double wire. This eliminates any overhead frogs (a potential cause of difficulty). As a bonus the real tramways used sprung points and double wires extensively. Another aid to smoother running is to design the track so that, as far as possible, the curved part of the point is used in the trailing direction and the straight part in the facing direction (though I have to admit that I did not do this myself in the London layout!).

I have to say my own preference has always been for small layouts. I like to add detail and this is much more practical with a smaller layout. The size I tend to use for a continuous run is 4 feet by 20 inches. This fits into the back of a medium sized hatchback, I can keep it in the loft (with a 21 inch wide access) and there are no boards to have to join up. With this size it is practical to fit a double oval. On the other hand I have had great success with an end to end layout on two boards with a combined size of 8ft by 1ft and a dog bone layout with three boards, two 2ft square and one 4ft by 1ft.

However, the main thing about a layout is that it must excite you. After all you are the one who will be committing your time to it. So make sure it will meet what you want, not what I write about or what others tell you. It is for you to enjoy building and operating. So finally may I wish you good modelling.

On the 3ft gauge is this Manx Electric layout by Don Curry. The centenary of the Isle of Man tramway saw several fine layouts. On this one Don has managed to get many of the famous features onto a small space. Here is the Derby Castle depot; the shelter that was used by passengers transferring from the horse trams; and the row of shops and houses at Port Jack. At the other end of the layout is "Lady Isabella" the great Laxey water wheel.

For something a little different you could try trackless trams, or as they became known trolleybuses. This is the layout made by Tony Chlad. He used the Faller street system and power through the overhead to create an amazing trolleybus layout.

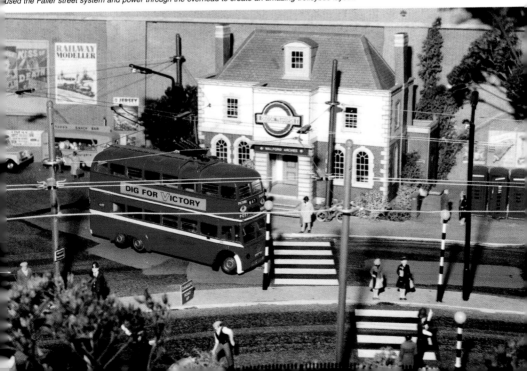

One of the most unusual tramcars to run in Britain was this early single deck four wheel tramcar and trailer from Liverpool. Known as the 'Chinese trams' from their distinctive curved cleristories the tramcars actually came from Germany. These are kits manufactured by Tramalan.

ABS have produced this lovely kit of the Hull enclosed tramcars. Several of this type of car were sold to Leeds where they became known as "Kipperboxes" from the fact that they came from Hull and had distinctive planked wooden dashes.

SOURCES OF INFORMATION AND SUPPLIERS OF 'OO' GAUGE TRAMWAYS

TRAMWAY AND LIGHT RAILWAY SOCIETY

The only national society for tramway modellers. All scales are welcomed, but there is a very active 'OO' gauge group. The society magazine "Tramfare" is sent to members six times a year. Articles on 'OO' gauge modelling regularly appear in the magazine.

For further details and an application form send an SAE to the Membership Secretary, J. Leach, 6, The Woodlands, Brightlingsea, Colchester, Essex, CO7 0RY.

MODEL TRAMWAY BOOKS

"Tramway Modelling in 'OO' Gauge". This is the companion volume to this book. The Chapters include tramway track; overhead wire construction and trouble shooting.

BOOKS ON PROTOTYPE TRAMWAYS

New Books

Lancastrian Transport Publications, 5, Rossall Road, Cleveleys, Blackpool, FY5 1AP. 01253 865324.

Ian Allan Transport Book Shop, 47, Stephenson Street, Birmingham, B2 4DH. 0121 643 2496.

Second-hand Books

Adam Gordon, Priory Cottage, Chetwode, Buckinghamshire, MK18 4LB, 01280 848650.

'OO' GAUGE TRAMWAY MODELLING SUPPLIERS

TLRS SHOP

A mail order service provided for TLRS members, mainly 'OO' gauge items including Alphagraphix and Model Tramcar System; but also some 'O' and 'G' gauge. For a catalogue send an SAE and 3 x first class stamps to Derek Lambelle, 18, Glanffrwyd Road, Glynhir, Pontardulais, Swansea, SA4 1QE. 01792 885997.

TRAMALAN

Manufacturer of white metal tramcar kits, tramway overhead and bogie mechanisms. Tramalan also provide a mail order service with all kinds of items for tramway modellers, mainly in 'OO' gauge. For catalogue send 6 x first class stamps to Tramalan, PO Box 2, Blackpool, FY3 8DZ.

TOWER MODELS

A retail model railway shop that specialises in tramway modelling. They manufacture their own plastic tramcar kits and offer other manufacturers kits and parts. Items are also available by mail order. Contact Tower Models, 44, Cookson Street, Blackpool, FY1 3ED. 01253 23797.

'OO' GAUGE TRAM KIT MANUFACTURERS

Tramalan, a range of British outline white metal kits.

ABS Models, a range of British outline white metal tramcar kits.

BEC Models, a range of 'HO' continental kits and 'OO' gauge mechanisms.

Tower Models, a range of British outline plastic tramcar kits

Blackpool Plastics (Hadfields), a range of plastic tramcar kits based on Blackpool trams.

Mark Hughes Models, a range of British outline etched brass and white metal kits.

Knightwing Models (Keil Kraft), Plastic tramcar kit of an Edinburgh tram.

Monmouth Models, White metal kit of a Black Country Tividale tram.

Alphagraphix, full colour card kits of British and Continental tramcars.

TRANSFERS AND ADVERTISEMENTS

Lancastrian Transport Publications have a range of self adhesive advertisement for Blackpool trams. Lancastrian Transport Publications, 5, Rossall Road, Cleveleys, Blackpool, FY5 1AP. 01253 865324.

Mabex, a supplier of specialist model transport transfers. Mabex Products, 15, Coastguard Square, Barden Road, Eastbourne, East Sussex, BN22 7EE.

Tower Models sell the transfers found in their tram and bus kits as separate items. In addition they have a Blackpool trams transfer set. Tower Models, 44, Cookson Street, Blackpool, FY1 3ED. 01253 23797.

WORKING TRAMWAYS

NOTE The opening times of the museums may be limited and/or seasonal. Check before making a long trip.

Birkenhead Tramways, Woodside Ferry, Birkenhead Wirral. 0151 666 4010.

Capturing the full character of the Bristol open top tramcars is this kit from Tramalan. Running unchanged for many many years the Bristol tramcars gained fame all over the country. Alas the system closed as a result of enemy action in 1941.

A line up of all the various types of Feltham tramcars available as plastic kits from Tower Models.

Black Country Museum, working 3 ft 6 in gauge tramway and trolleybus route. Tipton Road, Dudley West Midlands.

Blackpool Tramways, Starr Gate to Fleetwood Lancashire, the depot is at Rigby Road, by Manchester Square.

Douglas Horse Trams, from the Pier Douglas to the Manx Electric Tramway at Summerland.

East Anglia Transport Museum, Chapel Road, Carlton Colville, Near Lowestoft, Suffolk.

Great Orme Tramway, cable tramway, Llandudno. 01492 870870.

Heaton Park Tramway, Heaton Park, Manchester.

Manchester Metrolink, Altrincham and Bury to Manchester centre.

Manx Electric Tramways, Isle of Man from Douglas to Ramsey. 01624 663366.

National Tramway Museum, Crich, Nr Matlock, Derbyshire. 01773 852565.

North of England Open Air Museum, Beamish, County Durham.

Seaton and District Electric Tramways, Seaton to Colyton, Seaton, Devon. 01297 21702

Sheffield Tramway, South Yorkshire Supertram, Several routes radiating from Sheffield City Centre. 0114 272 8282

Snaefell Mountain Railway, Isle of Man, Laxey to Snaefell Mountain top, 01624 663366.

Summerlee Heritage Centre, Coatbridge, Strathclyde, (East of Glasgow)

Telford Horsehay Steam Trust, short 2ft gauge steam tramway, Old Locomotive Shed Horsehay, near Telford, Shropshire.

Transperience, West Yorkshire Transport Museum Trust, Low Moor, Bradford, Yorkshire.

STATIC TRAMS

Birmingham Museum of Transport and Industry, Newhall Street, Birmingham.

Bradford Industrial Museum, Moorside Mills, Moorside Road, Bradford.

Glasgow Museum of Transport, Kelvin Hall, Dumbarton Road, Glasgow.

Gloucester Transport Museum, Longsmith Street, Gloucester.

Grampian Transport Museum, Alford, 25 miles west of Aberdeen.